50 Hearty Winter Soups for Cozy Nights

By: Kelly Johnson

Table of Contents

- Classic Chicken Noodle Soup
- Creamy Tomato Basil Soup
- Beef and Barley Soup
- Potato Leek Soup
- Split Pea Soup with Ham
- Butternut Squash Soup
- Lentil Soup
- French Onion Soup
- Roasted Carrot and Ginger Soup
- Mushroom Soup
- Chicken and Wild Rice Soup
- Broccoli Cheddar Soup
- Creamy Potato Soup
- Clam Chowder
- Vegetable Minestrone
- Creamy Cauliflower Soup
- Tortilla Soup
- Pumpkin Soup
- Chicken and Corn Chowder
- Kale and White Bean Soup
- Sausage and Kale Soup
- Sweet Potato and Chickpea Soup
- Italian Wedding Soup
- Beef and Vegetable Soup
- Creamy Spinach and Artichoke Soup
- Curried Butternut Squash Soup
- Sweet Potato and Black Bean Soup
- Chickpea and Spinach Soup
- Tomato and Roasted Red Pepper Soup
- Hungarian Goulash Soup
- Borscht
- Chicken and Dumpling Soup
- Minestrone with Pesto
- Italian Sausage and Potato Soup
- Mushroom and Barley Soup

- Red Lentil Soup
- Beef Stew Soup
- Thai Coconut Soup
- Smoked Salmon Chowder
- Zuppa Toscana
- Cabbage and Sausage Soup
- Roasted Tomato Soup
- Cajun Chicken and Sausage Soup
- Moroccan Lentil Soup
- Spicy Black Bean Soup
- Fish Chowder
- Pumpkin and Sausage Soup
- Eggplant and Chickpea Soup
- Chicken Tortellini Soup
- Curried Carrot Soup

Classic Chicken Noodle Soup

Ingredients:

- 2 tbsp olive oil
- 1 medium onion, diced
- 2 carrots, sliced
- 2 celery stalks, diced
- 3 garlic cloves, minced
- 6 cups chicken broth
- 2 cups cooked chicken, shredded
- 2 cups egg noodles
- 1 tsp dried thyme
- 1/2 tsp dried rosemary
- Salt and pepper to taste
- Fresh parsley for garnish

Instructions:

1. **Sauté the vegetables**:
   Heat olive oil in a large pot over medium heat. Add the onion, carrots, and celery, and sauté until softened, about 5-7 minutes. Add garlic and cook for an additional minute.
2. **Simmer the soup**:
   Add the chicken broth, shredded chicken, thyme, and rosemary to the pot. Bring the mixture to a boil, then reduce the heat and let it simmer for 15 minutes.
3. **Cook the noodles**:
   Add the egg noodles to the soup and cook for about 10 minutes, or until the noodles are tender. Season with salt and pepper to taste.
4. **Serve**:
   Ladle the soup into bowls and garnish with fresh parsley. Serve hot.

Creamy Tomato Basil Soup

Ingredients:

- 2 tbsp butter
- 1 medium onion, chopped
- 2 garlic cloves, minced
- 2 cans (14.5 oz each) diced tomatoes
- 2 cups chicken broth
- 1 cup heavy cream
- 1 tsp sugar
- 1/2 tsp salt
- 1/4 tsp black pepper
- 1/4 cup fresh basil, chopped

Instructions:

1. **Sauté the onion and garlic**:
   In a large pot, melt the butter over medium heat. Add the onion and sauté until softened, about 5 minutes. Add the garlic and cook for another minute.
2. **Cook the soup base**:
   Add the diced tomatoes (with juice), chicken broth, sugar, salt, and pepper. Bring to a simmer and cook for 15 minutes.
3. **Blend the soup**:
   Use an immersion blender to puree the soup until smooth (or blend in batches using a regular blender).
4. **Finish the soup**:
   Stir in the heavy cream and chopped basil. Let it simmer for an additional 5 minutes, then adjust seasoning as needed.
5. **Serve**:
   Ladle the soup into bowls and garnish with extra basil leaves if desired.

Beef and Barley Soup

Ingredients:

- 2 tbsp olive oil
- 1 lb beef stew meat, cut into cubes
- 1 medium onion, chopped
- 2 carrots, sliced
- 2 celery stalks, chopped
- 3 garlic cloves, minced
- 6 cups beef broth
- 1 cup barley
- 1 bay leaf
- 1 tsp dried thyme
- Salt and pepper to taste
- Fresh parsley for garnish

Instructions:

1. **Brown the beef**:
   Heat olive oil in a large pot over medium-high heat. Add the beef stew meat and cook until browned on all sides, about 5-7 minutes. Remove the beef and set it aside.
2. **Sauté the vegetables**:
   In the same pot, add the onion, carrots, and celery, and sauté for about 5 minutes until softened. Add the garlic and cook for another minute.
3. **Cook the soup**:
   Add the beef back into the pot, followed by the beef broth, barley, bay leaf, thyme, salt, and pepper. Bring to a boil, then reduce the heat and simmer for about 45 minutes, or until the beef is tender and the barley is cooked.
4. **Serve**:
   Remove the bay leaf, ladle the soup into bowls, and garnish with fresh parsley.

Potato Leek Soup

Ingredients:

- 2 tbsp butter
- 3 leeks, cleaned and sliced
- 2 garlic cloves, minced
- 4 cups chicken broth
- 4 medium potatoes, peeled and diced
- 1 cup heavy cream
- Salt and pepper to taste
- Fresh chives for garnish

Instructions:

1. **Sauté the leeks and garlic:**
   In a large pot, melt the butter over medium heat. Add the leeks and sauté until softened, about 5-7 minutes. Add the garlic and cook for another minute.
2. **Simmer the soup:**
   Add the chicken broth and potatoes to the pot. Bring to a boil, then reduce the heat and simmer for about 20 minutes, or until the potatoes are tender.
3. **Blend the soup:**
   Use an immersion blender to puree the soup until smooth (or blend in batches using a regular blender).
4. **Finish the soup:**
   Stir in the heavy cream and season with salt and pepper to taste. Simmer for an additional 5 minutes.
5. **Serve:**
   Ladle the soup into bowls and garnish with fresh chives.

Split Pea Soup with Ham

Ingredients:

- 2 tbsp olive oil
- 1 onion, chopped
- 2 carrots, sliced
- 2 celery stalks, chopped
- 2 garlic cloves, minced
- 1 lb dried split peas
- 6 cups chicken broth
- 2 cups ham, cubed
- 1 bay leaf
- 1 tsp dried thyme
- Salt and pepper to taste

Instructions:

1. **Sauté the vegetables**:
   In a large pot, heat olive oil over medium heat. Add the onion, carrots, and celery, and sauté for about 5-7 minutes until softened. Add the garlic and cook for another minute.
2. **Cook the soup**:
   Add the split peas, chicken broth, ham, bay leaf, thyme, salt, and pepper. Bring to a boil, then reduce the heat and simmer for 1-1.5 hours, or until the peas are tender and the soup has thickened.
3. **Serve**:
   Remove the bay leaf, ladle the soup into bowls, and serve hot.

Butternut Squash Soup

Ingredients:

- 2 tbsp olive oil
- 1 medium onion, chopped
- 2 garlic cloves, minced
- 1 medium butternut squash, peeled and cubed
- 4 cups vegetable broth
- 1/2 tsp ground nutmeg
- Salt and pepper to taste
- 1/2 cup coconut milk (optional)

Instructions:

1. **Sauté the vegetables**:
   Heat olive oil in a large pot over medium heat. Add the onion and cook for 5 minutes, then add the garlic and cook for another minute.
2. **Cook the squash**:
   Add the cubed butternut squash and vegetable broth to the pot. Bring to a boil, then reduce the heat and simmer for 20-25 minutes, or until the squash is tender.
3. **Blend the soup**:
   Use an immersion blender to puree the soup until smooth (or blend in batches using a regular blender).
4. **Finish the soup**:
   Stir in the nutmeg, salt, pepper, and coconut milk if using. Simmer for an additional 5 minutes.
5. **Serve**:
   Ladle the soup into bowls and serve hot.

Lentil Soup

Ingredients:

- 2 tbsp olive oil
- 1 onion, chopped
- 2 carrots, sliced
- 2 celery stalks, chopped
- 2 garlic cloves, minced
- 1 cup dried lentils, rinsed
- 6 cups vegetable broth
- 1 bay leaf
- 1 tsp cumin
- 1/2 tsp turmeric
- Salt and pepper to taste
- Fresh parsley for garnish

Instructions:

1. **Sauté the vegetables**:
   Heat olive oil in a large pot over medium heat. Add the onion, carrots, and celery, and sauté for about 5-7 minutes until softened. Add the garlic and cook for another minute.
2. **Simmer the soup**:
   Add the lentils, vegetable broth, bay leaf, cumin, turmeric, salt, and pepper to the pot. Bring to a boil, then reduce the heat and simmer for 30-40 minutes, or until the lentils are tender.
3. **Serve**:
   Remove the bay leaf, ladle the soup into bowls, and garnish with fresh parsley.

French Onion Soup

Ingredients:

- 3 tbsp butter
- 4 large onions, thinly sliced
- 2 garlic cloves, minced
- 4 cups beef broth
- 1/2 cup white wine
- 1 tbsp fresh thyme, chopped
- Salt and pepper to taste
- 4 slices French baguette
- 1 1/2 cups grated Gruyère cheese

Instructions:

1. **Caramelize the onions**:
   In a large pot, melt the butter over medium heat. Add the onions and cook, stirring occasionally, until golden brown and caramelized, about 25 minutes.
2. **Simmer the soup**:
   Add the garlic and cook for another minute. Add the beef broth, white wine, thyme, salt, and pepper. Bring to a boil, then reduce the heat and simmer for 15-20 minutes.
3. **Broil the baguette**:
   Toast the baguette slices in the oven or on a grill until crispy. Place the slices on top of the soup in bowls, then top with grated Gruyère cheese.
4. **Finish the soup**:
   Place the bowls under the broiler for 2-3 minutes until the cheese is melted and bubbly. Serve hot.

Roasted Carrot and Ginger Soup

Ingredients:

- 2 tbsp olive oil
- 6 large carrots, peeled and chopped
- 1 medium onion, chopped
- 2 garlic cloves, minced
- 1-inch piece fresh ginger, grated
- 4 cups vegetable broth
- 1/2 tsp ground cumin
- Salt and pepper to taste
- 1/2 cup coconut milk (optional)

Instructions:

1. **Roast the carrots**:
   Preheat the oven to 400°F (200°C). Toss the chopped carrots with olive oil, salt, and pepper, then roast on a baking sheet for 25-30 minutes, or until tender.
2. **Sauté the onion and garlic**:
   In a large pot, sauté the onion in olive oil until softened, about 5 minutes. Add the garlic and grated ginger, and cook for another minute.
3. **Simmer the soup**:
   Add the roasted carrots, vegetable broth, cumin, salt, and pepper to the pot. Bring to a boil, then reduce the heat and simmer for 10 minutes.
4. **Blend the soup**:
   Use an immersion blender to puree the soup until smooth (or blend in batches using a regular blender). Stir in coconut milk if using.
5. **Serve**:
   Ladle the soup into bowls and serve hot.

Mushroom Soup

Ingredients:

- 2 tbsp butter
- 1 medium onion, chopped
- 2 garlic cloves, minced
- 1 lb mushrooms, sliced (any variety)
- 4 cups vegetable or chicken broth
- 1 cup heavy cream
- 1 tsp fresh thyme, chopped
- Salt and pepper to taste
- Fresh parsley for garnish

Instructions:

1. **Sauté the vegetables**:
   Heat butter in a large pot over medium heat. Add the onion and cook until softened, about 5 minutes. Add garlic and cook for another minute.
2. **Cook the mushrooms**:
   Add the mushrooms to the pot and sauté until they release their moisture and start to brown, about 10 minutes.
3. **Simmer the soup**:
   Pour in the broth and bring the soup to a simmer. Let it cook for about 15 minutes to develop the flavors.
4. **Blend the soup**:
   Use an immersion blender to blend the soup until smooth, or blend in batches using a regular blender.
5. **Finish the soup**:
   Stir in the heavy cream and thyme, and season with salt and pepper to taste. Let it simmer for an additional 5 minutes.
6. **Serve**:
   Ladle the soup into bowls, garnish with parsley, and serve hot.

Chicken and Wild Rice Soup

Ingredients:

- 2 tbsp olive oil
- 1 medium onion, chopped
- 2 carrots, diced
- 2 celery stalks, chopped
- 3 garlic cloves, minced
- 6 cups chicken broth
- 1 cup wild rice
- 2 cups cooked chicken, shredded
- 1 tsp dried thyme
- 1/2 tsp salt
- 1/4 tsp pepper
- 1 cup heavy cream

Instructions:

1. **Sauté the vegetables**:
   In a large pot, heat olive oil over medium heat. Add the onion, carrots, and celery, and sauté for about 5 minutes. Add garlic and cook for another minute.
2. **Cook the soup**:
   Add the chicken broth, wild rice, thyme, salt, and pepper to the pot. Bring to a boil, then reduce the heat and simmer for 30 minutes, or until the rice is tender.
3. **Add chicken and cream**:
   Stir in the shredded chicken and heavy cream, and cook for an additional 10 minutes.
4. **Serve**:
   Ladle the soup into bowls and serve hot.

Broccoli Cheddar Soup

Ingredients:

- 2 tbsp butter
- 1 medium onion, chopped
- 2 garlic cloves, minced
- 4 cups broccoli florets
- 4 cups chicken or vegetable broth
- 2 cups shredded cheddar cheese
- 1 cup heavy cream
- Salt and pepper to taste

Instructions:

1. **Sauté the onion and garlic**:
   In a large pot, melt the butter over medium heat. Add the onion and cook until softened, about 5 minutes. Add the garlic and cook for another minute.
2. **Cook the broccoli**:
   Add the broccoli and broth to the pot. Bring the soup to a boil, then reduce the heat and simmer for about 15-20 minutes, or until the broccoli is tender.
3. **Blend the soup**:
   Use an immersion blender to blend the soup until smooth, or blend in batches using a regular blender.
4. **Add the cheese and cream**:
   Stir in the shredded cheddar cheese and heavy cream. Cook for another 5 minutes, or until the cheese is melted.
5. **Serve**:
   Season with salt and pepper, and serve hot.

Creamy Potato Soup

Ingredients:

- 2 tbsp butter
- 1 medium onion, chopped
- 3 garlic cloves, minced
- 4 medium potatoes, peeled and diced
- 4 cups chicken or vegetable broth
- 1 cup heavy cream
- 1 tsp dried thyme
- Salt and pepper to taste
- Fresh chives for garnish

Instructions:

1. **Sauté the onion and garlic**:
   In a large pot, melt the butter over medium heat. Add the onion and cook until softened, about 5 minutes. Add the garlic and cook for another minute.
2. **Cook the potatoes**:
   Add the potatoes and broth to the pot. Bring to a boil, then reduce the heat and simmer for 20-25 minutes, or until the potatoes are tender.
3. **Blend the soup**:
   Use an immersion blender to blend the soup until smooth, or blend in batches using a regular blender.
4. **Add cream and seasonings**:
   Stir in the heavy cream, thyme, salt, and pepper, and cook for an additional 5 minutes.
5. **Serve**:
   Ladle the soup into bowls, garnish with chives, and serve hot.

Clam Chowder

Ingredients:

- 2 tbsp butter
- 1 medium onion, chopped
- 2 celery stalks, chopped
- 2 garlic cloves, minced
- 4 cups chicken or vegetable broth
- 2 cups potatoes, peeled and diced
- 2 cans (6.5 oz each) chopped clams, drained
- 1 cup heavy cream
- Salt and pepper to taste
- Fresh parsley for garnish

Instructions:

1. **Sauté the vegetables**:
   In a large pot, melt the butter over medium heat. Add the onion, celery, and garlic, and sauté for about 5 minutes until softened.
2. **Cook the potatoes**:
   Add the broth and potatoes to the pot. Bring to a boil, then reduce the heat and simmer for 15-20 minutes, or until the potatoes are tender.
3. **Add the clams and cream**:
   Stir in the clams and heavy cream, and cook for another 5 minutes.
4. **Serve**:
   Season with salt and pepper, garnish with fresh parsley, and serve hot.

Vegetable Minestrone

Ingredients:

- 2 tbsp olive oil
- 1 medium onion, chopped
- 2 carrots, diced
- 2 celery stalks, chopped
- 3 garlic cloves, minced
- 1 zucchini, diced
- 1 cup green beans, chopped
- 1 can (14.5 oz) diced tomatoes
- 4 cups vegetable broth
- 1/2 cup pasta (small shapes like ditalini or elbow)
- 1 tsp dried basil
- Salt and pepper to taste
- Fresh parsley for garnish

Instructions:

1. **Sauté the vegetables**:
   In a large pot, heat olive oil over medium heat. Add the onion, carrots, and celery, and sauté for about 5 minutes. Add garlic and cook for another minute.
2. **Simmer the soup**:
   Add the zucchini, green beans, tomatoes, broth, pasta, basil, salt, and pepper. Bring to a boil, then reduce the heat and simmer for 15-20 minutes, or until the vegetables are tender and the pasta is cooked.
3. **Serve**:
   Ladle the soup into bowls, garnish with fresh parsley, and serve hot.

Creamy Cauliflower Soup

Ingredients:

- 2 tbsp olive oil
- 1 medium onion, chopped
- 3 garlic cloves, minced
- 1 head cauliflower, cut into florets
- 4 cups vegetable broth
- 1 cup heavy cream
- Salt and pepper to taste
- Fresh thyme for garnish

Instructions:

1. **Sauté the onion and garlic**:
   In a large pot, heat olive oil over medium heat. Add the onion and cook until softened, about 5 minutes. Add the garlic and cook for another minute.
2. **Cook the cauliflower**:
   Add the cauliflower and broth to the pot. Bring to a boil, then reduce the heat and simmer for 15-20 minutes, or until the cauliflower is tender.
3. **Blend the soup**:
   Use an immersion blender to blend the soup until smooth, or blend in batches using a regular blender.
4. **Add the cream**:
   Stir in the heavy cream and season with salt and pepper to taste. Cook for an additional 5 minutes.
5. **Serve**:
   Ladle the soup into bowls, garnish with fresh thyme, and serve hot.

Tortilla Soup

Ingredients:

- 2 tbsp olive oil
- 1 medium onion, chopped
- 2 garlic cloves, minced
- 1 can (14.5 oz) diced tomatoes
- 4 cups chicken broth
- 1 tsp ground cumin
- 1/2 tsp chili powder
- 1 cup corn kernels
- 2 cups cooked chicken, shredded
- 1/4 cup cilantro, chopped
- 4 tortillas, cut into strips
- Fresh lime for garnish

Instructions:

1. **Sauté the onion and garlic**:
   In a large pot, heat olive oil over medium heat. Add the onion and cook until softened, about 5 minutes. Add garlic and cook for another minute.
2. **Cook the soup**:
   Add the tomatoes, chicken broth, cumin, chili powder, corn, chicken, and cilantro. Bring to a boil, then reduce the heat and simmer for 15-20 minutes.
3. **Fry the tortilla strips**:
   In a separate pan, heat some oil and fry the tortilla strips until crispy. Set them aside to drain on paper towels.
4. **Serve**:
   Ladle the soup into bowls, top with tortilla strips, and garnish with fresh lime.

Pumpkin Soup

Ingredients:

- 2 tbsp olive oil
- 1 medium onion, chopped
- 2 garlic cloves, minced
- 4 cups pumpkin puree
- 4 cups vegetable broth
- 1/2 tsp ground cinnamon
- 1/4 tsp nutmeg
- Salt and pepper to taste
- 1 cup heavy cream

Instructions:

1. **Sauté the onion and garlic:**
   In a large pot, heat olive oil over medium heat. Add the onion and cook until softened, about 5 minutes. Add garlic and cook for another minute.
2. **Cook the pumpkin:**
   Add the pumpkin puree, broth, cinnamon, nutmeg, salt, and pepper to the pot. Bring to a boil, then reduce the heat and simmer for 15 minutes.
3. **Finish the soup:**
   Stir in the heavy cream and cook for another 5 minutes.
4. **Serve:**
   Ladle the soup into bowls and serve hot.

Chicken and Corn Chowder

Ingredients:

- 2 tbsp butter
- 1 medium onion, chopped
- 2 garlic cloves, minced
- 3 medium potatoes, peeled and diced
- 4 cups chicken broth
- 2 cups cooked chicken, shredded
- 1 can (15 oz) corn kernels, drained
- 1 cup heavy cream
- Salt and pepper to taste
- Fresh parsley for garnish

Instructions:

1. **Sauté the onion and garlic:**
   In a large pot, melt the butter over medium heat. Add the onion and cook until softened, about 5 minutes. Add the garlic and cook for another minute.
2. **Cook the potatoes:**
   Add the potatoes and chicken broth to the pot. Bring to a boil, then reduce the heat and simmer for 15-20 minutes, or until the potatoes are tender.
3. **Add chicken and corn:**
   Stir in the shredded chicken and corn, and cook for an additional 5 minutes.
4. **Finish with cream:**
   Stir in the heavy cream and season with salt and pepper to taste. Let it simmer for another 5 minutes.
5. **Serve:**
   Ladle the chowder into bowls, garnish with fresh parsley, and serve hot.

Kale and White Bean Soup

Ingredients:

- 2 tbsp olive oil
- 1 medium onion, chopped
- 2 garlic cloves, minced
- 2 cups chopped kale
- 1 can (15 oz) white beans, drained and rinsed
- 4 cups vegetable broth
- 1 tsp dried thyme
- Salt and pepper to taste
- Fresh lemon juice (optional)

Instructions:

1. **Sauté the onion and garlic:**
   In a large pot, heat olive oil over medium heat. Add the onion and cook until softened, about 5 minutes. Add the garlic and cook for another minute.
2. **Simmer the soup:**
   Add the kale, white beans, vegetable broth, and thyme. Bring the soup to a boil, then reduce the heat and simmer for 15-20 minutes.
3. **Season the soup:**
   Season with salt, pepper, and a squeeze of fresh lemon juice if desired.
4. **Serve:**
   Ladle the soup into bowls and serve hot.

Sausage and Kale Soup

Ingredients:

- 2 tbsp olive oil
- 1 lb Italian sausage (mild or spicy), casings removed
- 1 medium onion, chopped
- 2 garlic cloves, minced
- 4 cups chicken broth
- 2 cups chopped kale
- 2 medium potatoes, peeled and diced
- 1 tsp dried oregano
- Salt and pepper to taste

Instructions:

1. **Brown the sausage**:
   In a large pot, heat olive oil over medium heat. Add the sausage and cook, breaking it up into pieces, until browned, about 5-7 minutes.
2. **Sauté the onion and garlic**:
   Add the onion and cook until softened, about 5 minutes. Add the garlic and cook for another minute.
3. **Simmer the soup**:
   Add the chicken broth, kale, potatoes, and oregano. Bring to a boil, then reduce the heat and simmer for 20-25 minutes, or until the potatoes are tender.
4. **Season the soup**:
   Season with salt and pepper to taste.
5. **Serve**:
   Ladle the soup into bowls and serve hot.

Sweet Potato and Chickpea Soup

Ingredients:

- 2 tbsp olive oil
- 1 medium onion, chopped
- 2 garlic cloves, minced
- 2 medium sweet potatoes, peeled and diced
- 1 can (15 oz) chickpeas, drained and rinsed
- 4 cups vegetable broth
- 1 tsp ground cumin
- 1/2 tsp ground coriander
- 1/4 tsp ground turmeric
- Salt and pepper to taste
- Fresh cilantro for garnish

Instructions:

1. **Sauté the onion and garlic:**
   In a large pot, heat olive oil over medium heat. Add the onion and cook until softened, about 5 minutes. Add the garlic and cook for another minute.
2. **Cook the sweet potatoes and chickpeas:**
   Add the sweet potatoes, chickpeas, vegetable broth, cumin, coriander, turmeric, salt, and pepper. Bring the soup to a boil, then reduce the heat and simmer for 20-25 minutes, or until the sweet potatoes are tender.
3. **Blend the soup:**
   Use an immersion blender to blend the soup until smooth, or blend in batches using a regular blender.
4. **Serve:**
   Ladle the soup into bowls and garnish with fresh cilantro. Serve hot.

Italian Wedding Soup

Ingredients:

- 2 tbsp olive oil
- 1 medium onion, chopped
- 2 garlic cloves, minced
- 4 cups chicken broth
- 1 cup baby spinach, chopped
- 1/2 cup small pasta (like orzo or acini di pepe)
- 1/2 lb ground beef or turkey
- 1/4 cup grated Parmesan cheese
- 1/4 cup breadcrumbs
- 1 egg, beaten
- Salt and pepper to taste

Instructions:

1. **Make the meatballs**:
   In a bowl, combine the ground meat, Parmesan cheese, breadcrumbs, egg, salt, and pepper. Form the mixture into small meatballs, about 1-inch in diameter.
2. **Cook the meatballs**:
   In a large pot, heat olive oil over medium heat. Add the meatballs and cook until browned, about 5 minutes. Remove the meatballs from the pot and set aside.
3. **Sauté the onion and garlic**:
   In the same pot, add the onion and cook until softened, about 5 minutes. Add the garlic and cook for another minute.
4. **Simmer the soup**:
   Add the chicken broth and bring to a boil. Add the pasta, cooked meatballs, and spinach. Reduce the heat and simmer for 10-15 minutes, or until the pasta is cooked.
5. **Serve**:
   Ladle the soup into bowls and serve hot.

Beef and Vegetable Soup

Ingredients:

- 2 tbsp olive oil
- 1 lb beef stew meat, cubed
- 1 medium onion, chopped
- 2 garlic cloves, minced
- 4 cups beef broth
- 3 carrots, sliced
- 2 celery stalks, chopped
- 2 medium potatoes, peeled and diced
- 1 can (14.5 oz) diced tomatoes
- 1 tsp dried thyme
- Salt and pepper to taste

Instructions:

1. **Brown the beef:**
   In a large pot, heat olive oil over medium heat. Add the beef stew meat and cook until browned on all sides, about 5-7 minutes.
2. **Sauté the onion and garlic:**
   Add the onion and cook until softened, about 5 minutes. Add the garlic and cook for another minute.
3. **Simmer the soup:**
   Add the beef broth, carrots, celery, potatoes, tomatoes, thyme, salt, and pepper. Bring the soup to a boil, then reduce the heat and simmer for 30-40 minutes, or until the vegetables are tender and the beef is cooked.
4. **Serve:**
   Ladle the soup into bowls and serve hot.

Creamy Spinach and Artichoke Soup

Ingredients:

- 2 tbsp butter
- 1 medium onion, chopped
- 2 garlic cloves, minced
- 1 can (14.5 oz) artichoke hearts, drained and chopped
- 4 cups vegetable broth
- 2 cups fresh spinach, chopped
- 1 cup heavy cream
- 1/2 cup grated Parmesan cheese
- Salt and pepper to taste

Instructions:

1. **Sauté the onion and garlic:**
   In a large pot, melt the butter over medium heat. Add the onion and cook until softened, about 5 minutes. Add the garlic and cook for another minute.
2. **Cook the artichokes and spinach:**
   Add the artichokes, vegetable broth, spinach, and cook for 5 minutes until the spinach is wilted.
3. **Finish with cream and Parmesan:**
   Stir in the heavy cream and Parmesan cheese. Simmer for another 5 minutes.
4. **Serve:**
   Season with salt and pepper to taste, and serve hot.

Curried Butternut Squash Soup

Ingredients:

- 2 tbsp olive oil
- 1 medium onion, chopped
- 2 garlic cloves, minced
- 1 medium butternut squash, peeled and cubed
- 4 cups vegetable broth
- 1 tsp ground curry powder
- 1/2 tsp ground ginger
- Salt and pepper to taste
- 1 cup coconut milk

Instructions:

1. **Sauté the onion and garlic**:
   In a large pot, heat olive oil over medium heat. Add the onion and cook until softened, about 5 minutes. Add the garlic and cook for another minute.
2. **Cook the squash**:
   Add the butternut squash, vegetable broth, curry powder, ginger, salt, and pepper. Bring to a boil, then reduce the heat and simmer for 20-25 minutes, or until the squash is tender.
3. **Blend the soup**:
   Use an immersion blender to blend the soup until smooth, or blend in batches using a regular blender.
4. **Finish with coconut milk**:
   Stir in the coconut milk and simmer for another 5 minutes.
5. **Serve**:
   Ladle the soup into bowls and serve hot.

Sweet Potato and Black Bean Soup

Ingredients:

- 2 tbsp olive oil
- 1 medium onion, chopped
- 2 garlic cloves, minced
- 2 medium sweet potatoes, peeled and diced
- 1 can (15 oz) black beans, drained and rinsed
- 4 cups vegetable broth
- 1 tsp ground cumin
- 1/2 tsp ground chili powder
- Salt and pepper to taste
- Fresh cilantro for garnish
- Lime wedges for serving

Instructions:

1. **Sauté the onion and garlic**:
   In a large pot, heat olive oil over medium heat. Add the onion and cook until softened, about 5 minutes. Add the garlic and cook for another minute.
2. **Cook the sweet potatoes**:
   Add the sweet potatoes, black beans, vegetable broth, cumin, chili powder, salt, and pepper. Bring to a boil, then reduce the heat and simmer for 20-25 minutes, or until the sweet potatoes are tender.
3. **Blend the soup**:
   Use an immersion blender to blend the soup until smooth, or blend in batches using a regular blender.
4. **Serve**:
   Ladle the soup into bowls, garnish with fresh cilantro, and serve with lime wedges.

Chickpea and Spinach Soup

Ingredients:

- 2 tbsp olive oil
- 1 medium onion, chopped
- 2 garlic cloves, minced
- 1 can (15 oz) chickpeas, drained and rinsed
- 4 cups vegetable broth
- 2 cups fresh spinach, chopped
- 1 tsp ground cumin
- 1/2 tsp ground coriander
- 1/4 tsp ground turmeric
- Salt and pepper to taste

Instructions:

1. **Sauté the onion and garlic**:
   In a large pot, heat olive oil over medium heat. Add the onion and cook until softened, about 5 minutes. Add the garlic and cook for another minute.
2. **Simmer the soup**:
   Add the chickpeas, vegetable broth, spinach, cumin, coriander, turmeric, salt, and pepper. Bring the soup to a boil, then reduce the heat and simmer for 15-20 minutes.
3. **Blend if desired**:
   For a smoother soup, use an immersion blender to blend the soup to your desired consistency.
4. **Serve**:
   Ladle the soup into bowls and serve hot.

Tomato and Roasted Red Pepper Soup

Ingredients:

- 2 tbsp olive oil
- 1 medium onion, chopped
- 2 garlic cloves, minced
- 2 red bell peppers, roasted, peeled, and chopped
- 2 cans (15 oz each) crushed tomatoes
- 4 cups vegetable broth
- 1 tsp dried basil
- 1/2 tsp ground thyme
- Salt and pepper to taste
- 1/2 cup heavy cream (optional)

Instructions:

1. **Sauté the onion and garlic**:
   In a large pot, heat olive oil over medium heat. Add the onion and cook until softened, about 5 minutes. Add the garlic and cook for another minute.
2. **Add the roasted peppers and tomatoes**:
   Add the roasted red peppers, crushed tomatoes, vegetable broth, basil, thyme, salt, and pepper. Bring the soup to a boil, then reduce the heat and simmer for 15-20 minutes.
3. **Blend the soup**:
   Use an immersion blender to blend the soup until smooth, or blend in batches using a regular blender.
4. **Finish with cream**:
   Stir in the heavy cream if desired, and simmer for an additional 5 minutes.
5. **Serve**:
   Ladle the soup into bowls and serve hot.

Hungarian Goulash Soup

Ingredients:

- 2 tbsp olive oil
- 1 lb beef stew meat, cubed
- 1 medium onion, chopped
- 2 garlic cloves, minced
- 2 tbsp paprika (preferably Hungarian)
- 1 tsp caraway seeds (optional)
- 4 cups beef broth
- 2 medium potatoes, peeled and diced
- 2 carrots, sliced
- 1 can (14.5 oz) diced tomatoes
- Salt and pepper to taste
- Fresh parsley for garnish

Instructions:

1. **Brown the beef**:
   In a large pot, heat olive oil over medium heat. Add the beef stew meat and cook until browned on all sides, about 5-7 minutes. Remove the beef and set aside.
2. **Sauté the onion and garlic**:
   In the same pot, add the onion and cook until softened, about 5 minutes. Add the garlic and paprika, and cook for another minute.
3. **Simmer the soup**:
   Add the beef broth, potatoes, carrots, diced tomatoes, caraway seeds, salt, and pepper. Bring the soup to a boil, then reduce the heat and simmer for 30-40 minutes, or until the vegetables are tender.
4. **Serve**:
   Ladle the soup into bowls, garnish with fresh parsley, and serve hot.

Borscht

Ingredients:

- 2 tbsp olive oil
- 1 medium onion, chopped
- 2 medium beets, peeled and grated
- 1 carrot, peeled and grated
- 2 garlic cloves, minced
- 4 cups vegetable broth
- 1 tbsp apple cider vinegar
- 1 tsp sugar
- Salt and pepper to taste
- 1/2 cup sour cream
- Fresh dill for garnish

Instructions:

1. **Sauté the onion and garlic:**
   In a large pot, heat olive oil over medium heat. Add the onion and cook until softened, about 5 minutes. Add the garlic and cook for another minute.
2. **Cook the beets and carrots:**
   Add the grated beets and carrots, and cook for 5 minutes, stirring occasionally.
3. **Simmer the soup:**
   Add the vegetable broth, apple cider vinegar, sugar, salt, and pepper. Bring the soup to a boil, then reduce the heat and simmer for 30-40 minutes, until the beets are tender.
4. **Finish and serve:**
   Stir in the sour cream and garnish with fresh dill. Serve hot.

Chicken and Dumpling Soup

Ingredients:

- 2 tbsp butter
- 1 medium onion, chopped
- 2 garlic cloves, minced
- 4 cups chicken broth
- 2 cups cooked, shredded chicken
- 1 cup carrots, sliced
- 1 cup celery, chopped
- 1 cup frozen peas
- 2 cups flour
- 2 tsp baking powder
- 1/2 tsp salt
- 1/2 tsp pepper
- 1 cup milk
- 1/4 cup chopped fresh parsley

Instructions:

1. **Sauté the onion and garlic:**
   In a large pot, melt butter over medium heat. Add the onion and cook until softened, about 5 minutes. Add the garlic and cook for another minute.
2. **Simmer the soup:**
   Add the chicken broth, shredded chicken, carrots, celery, and peas. Bring to a boil, then reduce the heat and simmer for 10 minutes.
3. **Make the dumplings:**
   In a bowl, mix together the flour, baking powder, salt, and pepper. Stir in the milk to form a thick batter. Drop spoonfuls of the batter into the simmering soup.
4. **Cook the dumplings:**
   Cover the pot and simmer for 15-20 minutes, or until the dumplings are cooked through.
5. **Serve:**
   Ladle the soup into bowls, garnish with fresh parsley, and serve hot.

Minestrone with Pesto

Ingredients:

- 2 tbsp olive oil
- 1 medium onion, chopped
- 2 garlic cloves, minced
- 2 carrots, sliced
- 2 celery stalks, chopped
- 1 can (15 oz) diced tomatoes
- 4 cups vegetable broth
- 1 cup pasta (small shapes like elbow macaroni)
- 1 can (15 oz) kidney beans, drained and rinsed
- 1 zucchini, chopped
- 1 cup spinach, chopped
- 1/4 cup pesto
- Salt and pepper to taste

Instructions:

1. **Sauté the onion and garlic**:
   In a large pot, heat olive oil over medium heat. Add the onion and cook until softened, about 5 minutes. Add the garlic and cook for another minute.
2. **Simmer the soup**:
   Add the carrots, celery, diced tomatoes, vegetable broth, pasta, kidney beans, zucchini, and spinach. Bring to a boil, then reduce the heat and simmer for 15-20 minutes, or until the vegetables and pasta are tender.
3. **Finish with pesto**:
   Stir in the pesto, and season with salt and pepper to taste.
4. **Serve**:
   Ladle the soup into bowls and serve hot.

Italian Sausage and Potato Soup

Ingredients:

- 2 tbsp olive oil
- 1 lb Italian sausage (mild or spicy), casings removed
- 1 medium onion, chopped
- 2 garlic cloves, minced
- 4 cups chicken broth
- 3 medium potatoes, peeled and diced
- 1 cup kale or spinach, chopped
- 1/2 cup heavy cream
- Salt and pepper to taste

Instructions:

1. **Brown the sausage:**
   In a large pot, heat olive oil over medium heat. Add the sausage and cook until browned, breaking it up with a spoon.
2. **Sauté the onion and garlic:**
   Add the onion and cook until softened, about 5 minutes. Add the garlic and cook for another minute.
3. **Simmer the soup:**
   Add the chicken broth, potatoes, and kale or spinach. Bring to a boil, then reduce the heat and simmer for 20-25 minutes, or until the potatoes are tender.
4. **Finish the soup:**
   Stir in the heavy cream, and season with salt and pepper to taste.
5. **Serve:**
   Ladle the soup into bowls and serve hot.

Mushroom and Barley Soup

Ingredients:

- 2 tbsp olive oil
- 1 lb mushrooms, sliced
- 1 medium onion, chopped
- 2 garlic cloves, minced
- 4 cups vegetable broth
- 1 cup barley
- 2 carrots, sliced
- 1/2 tsp dried thyme
- Salt and pepper to taste
- Fresh parsley for garnish

Instructions:

1. **Sauté the mushrooms, onion, and garlic:**
   In a large pot, heat olive oil over medium heat. Add the mushrooms, onion, and garlic, and cook until softened, about 5-7 minutes.
2. **Simmer the soup**:
   Add the vegetable broth, barley, carrots, thyme, salt, and pepper. Bring to a boil, then reduce the heat and simmer for 30-40 minutes, or until the barley is tender.
3. **Serve**:
   Ladle the soup into bowls, garnish with fresh parsley, and serve hot.

Red Lentil Soup

Ingredients:

- 2 tbsp olive oil
- 1 medium onion, chopped
- 2 garlic cloves, minced
- 1 carrot, chopped
- 1 celery stalk, chopped
- 1 cup red lentils, rinsed
- 4 cups vegetable broth
- 1 can (14.5 oz) diced tomatoes
- 1 tsp ground cumin
- 1/2 tsp ground turmeric
- 1/2 tsp smoked paprika
- Salt and pepper to taste
- Fresh cilantro for garnish

Instructions:

1. **Sauté the vegetables:**
   In a large pot, heat olive oil over medium heat. Add the onion, carrot, and celery, and cook until softened, about 5 minutes. Add the garlic and cook for another minute.
2. **Add the lentils and seasonings:**
   Stir in the red lentils, cumin, turmeric, smoked paprika, salt, and pepper. Add the diced tomatoes and vegetable broth, and bring the soup to a boil.
3. **Simmer the soup:**
   Reduce the heat and simmer for 25-30 minutes, or until the lentils are soft and cooked through.
4. **Blend the soup** (optional):
   For a smooth soup, use an immersion blender to blend the soup until smooth.
5. **Serve:**
   Ladle the soup into bowls, garnish with fresh cilantro, and serve hot.

Beef Stew Soup

Ingredients:

- 2 tbsp olive oil
- 1 lb beef stew meat, cubed
- 1 medium onion, chopped
- 2 garlic cloves, minced
- 3 medium potatoes, peeled and diced
- 2 carrots, sliced
- 1 celery stalk, chopped
- 4 cups beef broth
- 1 tsp dried thyme
- 1 tsp ground paprika
- Salt and pepper to taste
- Fresh parsley for garnish

Instructions:

1. **Brown the beef:**
   In a large pot, heat olive oil over medium heat. Add the beef stew meat and brown on all sides, about 5-7 minutes. Remove the beef and set aside.
2. **Sauté the onion and garlic:**
   In the same pot, add the onion and cook until softened, about 5 minutes. Add the garlic and cook for another minute.
3. **Add the vegetables and broth:**
   Add the potatoes, carrots, celery, beef broth, thyme, paprika, salt, and pepper. Bring to a boil, then reduce the heat and simmer for 30-40 minutes, until the vegetables are tender.
4. **Finish the soup:**
   Return the browned beef to the pot and cook for an additional 10-15 minutes.
5. **Serve:**
   Ladle the soup into bowls and garnish with fresh parsley.

Thai Coconut Soup

Ingredients:

- 1 tbsp olive oil
- 1 medium onion, chopped
- 2 garlic cloves, minced
- 1-inch piece of ginger, grated
- 1 can (14 oz) coconut milk
- 4 cups chicken broth
- 1 lb chicken breasts, cooked and shredded
- 1 cup mushrooms, sliced
- 1 red bell pepper, chopped
- 1 tbsp fish sauce
- 1 tbsp lime juice
- 1 tsp brown sugar
- Fresh cilantro for garnish
- Lime wedges for serving

Instructions:

1. **Sauté the aromatics:**
   In a large pot, heat olive oil over medium heat. Add the onion and cook until softened, about 5 minutes. Add the garlic and ginger, and cook for another minute.
2. **Simmer the soup:**
   Add the coconut milk, chicken broth, shredded chicken, mushrooms, bell pepper, fish sauce, lime juice, and brown sugar. Bring the soup to a boil, then reduce the heat and simmer for 15-20 minutes.
3. **Serve:**
   Ladle the soup into bowls, garnish with fresh cilantro, and serve with lime wedges.

Smoked Salmon Chowder

Ingredients:

- 2 tbsp butter
- 1 medium onion, chopped
- 2 garlic cloves, minced
- 2 medium potatoes, peeled and diced
- 4 cups chicken broth
- 1 cup heavy cream
- 1/2 lb smoked salmon, chopped
- 1/2 cup frozen peas
- Salt and pepper to taste
- Fresh dill for garnish

Instructions:

1. **Sauté the onion and garlic:**
   In a large pot, melt butter over medium heat. Add the onion and cook until softened, about 5 minutes. Add the garlic and cook for another minute.
2. **Simmer the potatoes:**
   Add the potatoes and chicken broth to the pot. Bring the soup to a boil, then reduce the heat and simmer for 15-20 minutes, until the potatoes are tender.
3. **Finish the soup:**
   Stir in the heavy cream, smoked salmon, peas, salt, and pepper. Simmer for another 5 minutes.
4. **Serve:**
   Ladle the chowder into bowls and garnish with fresh dill.

Zuppa Toscana

Ingredients:

- 2 tbsp olive oil
- 1 lb Italian sausage, casings removed
- 1 medium onion, chopped
- 2 garlic cloves, minced
- 4 cups chicken broth
- 4 medium potatoes, sliced
- 1 bunch kale, chopped
- 1/2 cup heavy cream
- Salt and pepper to taste

Instructions:

1. **Brown the sausage:**
   In a large pot, heat olive oil over medium heat. Add the sausage and cook until browned, breaking it up with a spoon.
2. **Sauté the onion and garlic:**
   Add the onion and cook until softened, about 5 minutes. Add the garlic and cook for another minute.
3. **Simmer the soup:**
   Add the chicken broth, potatoes, kale, salt, and pepper. Bring to a boil, then reduce the heat and simmer for 20 minutes, or until the potatoes are tender.
4. **Finish with cream:**
   Stir in the heavy cream and simmer for another 5 minutes.
5. **Serve:**
   Ladle the soup into bowls and serve hot.

Cabbage and Sausage Soup

Ingredients:

- 2 tbsp olive oil
- 1 lb Italian sausage, casings removed
- 1 medium onion, chopped
- 2 garlic cloves, minced
- 4 cups chicken broth
- 1 small head cabbage, shredded
- 2 carrots, sliced
- 1 tsp dried thyme
- Salt and pepper to taste

Instructions:

1. **Brown the sausage**:
   In a large pot, heat olive oil over medium heat. Add the sausage and cook until browned, breaking it up with a spoon.
2. **Sauté the onion and garlic**:
   Add the onion and cook until softened, about 5 minutes. Add the garlic and cook for another minute.
3. **Simmer the soup**:
   Add the chicken broth, cabbage, carrots, thyme, salt, and pepper. Bring to a boil, then reduce the heat and simmer for 25-30 minutes, or until the cabbage is tender.
4. **Serve**:
   Ladle the soup into bowls and serve hot.

Roasted Tomato Soup

Ingredients:

- 2 tbsp olive oil
- 2 lbs tomatoes, halved
- 1 medium onion, chopped
- 2 garlic cloves, minced
- 4 cups vegetable broth
- 1 tsp dried basil
- 1/2 tsp sugar
- Salt and pepper to taste
- 1/2 cup heavy cream (optional)

Instructions:

1. **Roast the tomatoes**:
   Preheat the oven to 400°F (200°C). Place the tomato halves on a baking sheet, drizzle with olive oil, and season with salt and pepper. Roast for 25-30 minutes, until the tomatoes are soft and caramelized.
2. **Sauté the onion and garlic**:
   In a large pot, heat olive oil over medium heat. Add the onion and cook until softened, about 5 minutes. Add the garlic and cook for another minute.
3. **Simmer the soup**:
   Add the roasted tomatoes, vegetable broth, basil, sugar, salt, and pepper. Bring to a boil, then reduce the heat and simmer for 10 minutes.
4. **Blend the soup**:
   Use an immersion blender to blend the soup until smooth, or blend in batches using a regular blender.
5. **Finish with cream**:
   Stir in the heavy cream if desired.
6. **Serve**:
   Ladle the soup into bowls and serve hot.

Cajun Chicken and Sausage Soup

Ingredients:

- 2 tbsp olive oil
- 1 lb chicken breasts, cubed
- 1/2 lb smoked sausage, sliced
- 1 medium onion, chopped
- 2 garlic cloves, minced
- 1 red bell pepper, chopped
- 2 celery stalks, chopped
- 4 cups chicken broth
- 1 can (14.5 oz) diced tomatoes
- 1 tsp Cajun seasoning
- 1 tsp paprika
- Salt and pepper to taste

Instructions:

1. **Cook the chicken and sausage**:
   In a large pot, heat olive oil over medium heat. Add the chicken and sausage, and cook until the chicken is browned.
2. **Sauté the vegetables**:
   Add the onion, garlic, bell pepper, and celery, and cook for 5 minutes, until softened.
3. **Simmer the soup**:
   Add the chicken broth, diced tomatoes, Cajun seasoning, paprika, salt, and pepper. Bring to a boil, then reduce the heat and simmer for 20 minutes.
4. **Serve**:
   Ladle the soup into bowls and serve hot.

Moroccan Lentil Soup

Ingredients:

- 2 tbsp olive oil
- 1 medium onion, chopped
- 2 garlic cloves, minced
- 1 carrot, chopped
- 1 celery stalk, chopped
- 1 cup dried green or brown lentils, rinsed
- 4 cups vegetable broth
- 1 can (14.5 oz) diced tomatoes
- 1 tsp ground cumin
- 1 tsp ground coriander
- 1/2 tsp ground turmeric
- 1/4 tsp cinnamon
- 1/4 tsp ground ginger
- Salt and pepper to taste
- Fresh cilantro for garnish
- Lemon wedges for serving

Instructions:

1. **Sauté the vegetables**:
   In a large pot, heat olive oil over medium heat. Add the onion, carrot, and celery, and cook until softened, about 5-7 minutes. Add the garlic and cook for another minute.
2. **Add the lentils and spices**:
   Stir in the lentils, cumin, coriander, turmeric, cinnamon, and ginger. Season with salt and pepper.
3. **Simmer the soup**:
   Add the vegetable broth and diced tomatoes. Bring the soup to a boil, then reduce the heat and simmer for 30-35 minutes, or until the lentils are tender.
4. **Serve**:
   Ladle the soup into bowls, garnish with fresh cilantro, and serve with lemon wedges.

Spicy Black Bean Soup

Ingredients:

- 2 tbsp olive oil
- 1 medium onion, chopped
- 2 garlic cloves, minced
- 1 jalapeño pepper, minced (optional for extra heat)
- 2 cans (15 oz each) black beans, drained and rinsed
- 4 cups vegetable broth
- 1 can (14.5 oz) diced tomatoes
- 1 tsp ground cumin
- 1 tsp chili powder
- 1/2 tsp smoked paprika
- Salt and pepper to taste
- Fresh lime juice for garnish
- Sour cream or yogurt for topping (optional)

Instructions:

1. **Sauté the vegetables:**
   In a large pot, heat olive oil over medium heat. Add the onion and cook until softened, about 5 minutes. Add the garlic and jalapeño (if using), and cook for another minute.
2. **Simmer the soup:**
   Add the black beans, vegetable broth, diced tomatoes, cumin, chili powder, smoked paprika, salt, and pepper. Bring to a boil, then reduce the heat and simmer for 20-25 minutes.
3. **Blend the soup** (optional):
   For a smoother texture, use an immersion blender to blend the soup slightly, or blend half of the soup in a regular blender and return it to the pot.
4. **Serve:**
   Ladle the soup into bowls and garnish with fresh lime juice and a dollop of sour cream or yogurt, if desired.

Fish Chowder

Ingredients:

- 2 tbsp butter
- 1 lb white fish (cod, haddock, or tilapia), cut into cubes
- 1 medium onion, chopped
- 2 garlic cloves, minced
- 3 medium potatoes, peeled and diced
- 4 cups seafood or chicken broth
- 1 cup heavy cream
- 1 cup frozen corn
- 1/2 tsp thyme
- Salt and pepper to taste
- Fresh parsley for garnish

Instructions:

1. **Sauté the fish**:
   In a large pot, melt butter over medium heat. Add the fish and cook until lightly browned, about 5 minutes. Remove the fish and set aside.
2. **Cook the vegetables**:
   In the same pot, add the onion and cook until softened, about 5 minutes. Add the garlic and cook for another minute.
3. **Simmer the chowder**:
   Add the potatoes, broth, and thyme. Bring to a boil, then reduce the heat and simmer for 15 minutes, or until the potatoes are tender.
4. **Finish the soup**:
   Stir in the heavy cream, corn, salt, and pepper. Return the cooked fish to the pot and simmer for another 5 minutes.
5. **Serve**:
   Ladle the chowder into bowls and garnish with fresh parsley.

Pumpkin and Sausage Soup

Ingredients:

- 2 tbsp olive oil
- 1 lb Italian sausage, casings removed
- 1 medium onion, chopped
- 2 garlic cloves, minced
- 2 cups pumpkin puree
- 4 cups chicken broth
- 1 tsp ground sage
- 1/2 tsp ground cinnamon
- Salt and pepper to taste
- 1/2 cup heavy cream (optional)
- Fresh parsley for garnish

Instructions:

1. **Cook the sausage**:
   In a large pot, heat olive oil over medium heat. Add the sausage and cook, breaking it apart, until browned, about 5-7 minutes. Remove the sausage and set aside.
2. **Sauté the vegetables**:
   In the same pot, add the onion and cook until softened, about 5 minutes. Add the garlic and cook for another minute.
3. **Simmer the soup**:
   Add the pumpkin puree, chicken broth, sage, cinnamon, salt, and pepper. Bring to a boil, then reduce the heat and simmer for 15-20 minutes.
4. **Finish with cream**:
   Stir in the heavy cream if using and return the cooked sausage to the pot. Simmer for another 5 minutes.
5. **Serve**:
   Ladle the soup into bowls and garnish with fresh parsley.

Eggplant and Chickpea Soup

Ingredients:

- 2 tbsp olive oil
- 1 medium eggplant, cubed
- 1 medium onion, chopped
- 2 garlic cloves, minced
- 1 can (15 oz) chickpeas, drained and rinsed
- 4 cups vegetable broth
- 1 tsp ground cumin
- 1/2 tsp smoked paprika
- 1/4 tsp ground cinnamon
- Salt and pepper to taste
- Fresh cilantro for garnish

Instructions:

1. **Sauté the eggplant**:
   In a large pot, heat olive oil over medium heat. Add the cubed eggplant and cook until softened and lightly browned, about 8 minutes. Remove and set aside.
2. **Cook the aromatics**:
   Add the onion to the pot and cook until softened, about 5 minutes. Add the garlic and cook for another minute.
3. **Simmer the soup**:
   Add the chickpeas, vegetable broth, cumin, paprika, cinnamon, salt, and pepper. Bring to a boil, then reduce the heat and simmer for 20 minutes.
4. **Finish with eggplant**:
   Return the cooked eggplant to the pot and simmer for another 5 minutes.
5. **Serve**:
   Ladle the soup into bowls and garnish with fresh cilantro.

Chicken Tortellini Soup

Ingredients:

- 2 tbsp olive oil
- 1 lb chicken breasts, cooked and shredded
- 1 medium onion, chopped
- 2 garlic cloves, minced
- 4 cups chicken broth
- 1 can (14.5 oz) diced tomatoes
- 1 tsp dried thyme
- 1 tsp dried basil
- 1 package (9 oz) cheese tortellini
- Salt and pepper to taste
- Fresh spinach or kale for garnish

Instructions:

1. **Sauté the chicken**:
   In a large pot, heat olive oil over medium heat. Add the shredded chicken and cook for 2-3 minutes to warm through. Remove and set aside.
2. **Cook the aromatics**:
   Add the onion to the pot and cook until softened, about 5 minutes. Add the garlic and cook for another minute.
3. **Simmer the soup**:
   Add the chicken broth, diced tomatoes, thyme, basil, salt, and pepper. Bring to a boil, then reduce the heat and simmer for 15 minutes.
4. **Cook the tortellini**:
   Stir in the tortellini and cook according to package instructions, usually 5-7 minutes.
5. **Serve**:
   Ladle the soup into bowls and garnish with fresh spinach or kale.

Curried Carrot Soup

Ingredients:

- 2 tbsp olive oil
- 1 medium onion, chopped
- 2 garlic cloves, minced
- 1-inch piece ginger, grated
- 4 cups vegetable broth
- 6 medium carrots, peeled and chopped
- 1 tsp curry powder
- 1/2 tsp ground cumin
- Salt and pepper to taste
- 1/2 cup coconut milk (optional)
- Fresh cilantro for garnish

Instructions:

1. **Sauté the vegetables**:
   In a large pot, heat olive oil over medium heat. Add the onion and cook until softened, about 5 minutes. Add the garlic and ginger, and cook for another minute.
2. **Simmer the soup**:
   Add the carrots, vegetable broth, curry powder, cumin, salt, and pepper. Bring to a boil, then reduce the heat and simmer for 25-30 minutes, or until the carrots are tender.
3. **Blend the soup**:
   Use an immersion blender to blend the soup until smooth, or blend in batches using a regular blender.
4. **Finish with coconut milk**:
   Stir in the coconut milk (if using) and heat for another 5 minutes.
5. **Serve**:
   Ladle the soup into bowls and garnish with fresh cilantro.